National Council for Hospice and Specialist Palliative Care Services

Guidance for Managing Cancer Pain in Adults

Guidance for Managing Cancer Pain in Adults

This guidance has been developed by
a multiprofessional Working Party convened
by the National Council for Hospice and
Specialist Palliative Care Services.

The Working Party is grateful to
Janssen-Cilag and Napp Pharmaceuticals
for their support in the production of this document

Revised June 2003

Acknowledgements

Working Party members

Dr Teresa Tate (Chair), Medical Adviser, Marie Curie Cancer Care, Consultant in Palliative Medicine, Barts and the London NHS Trust

Dr Ian N Back, Consultant in Palliative Medicine, Y Bwthyn Palliative Care Unit, Pontypridd & Rhondda NHS Trust, Mid Glamorgan, Wales and Marie Curie Centre Holme Tower, Penarth, South Glamorgan, Wales

Margaret Fielding, Community Macmillan Nurse, Marlow Health Centre, Marlow

Dr Karen Forbes, Consultant and Macmillan Lecturer in Palliative Medicine, United Bristol Healthcare Trust and the University of Bristol

Bernadette Griffin, Cancer Nurse Specialist and Nurse Adviser, CancerBACUP, London

Dr Chris Higgs, Medical Director, Dorothy House Hospice, Nr Bath

Christine Hirsch, Research Pharmacist, Compton Hospice, West Midlands

Project Co-ordinator: Jayne Thomas, Projects Officer, National Council for Hospice and Specialist Palliative Care Services

Contents

Introduction   2

Cancer Pain   3

Aims of Management   5

Principles of Management   6

Pain Assessment   7

Pharmacological Management   9

   WHO Analgesic Ladder   9

   Morphine   11

   Alternative strong opioids   12

   Alternative routes of administration   15

   Breakthrough pain   17

   Opioid side effects   19

   Adjuvant treatments   24

Audit   27

References   27

This guidance reflects a fundamental principle of palliative care – patient-centred care applied across all conditions and in all settings. It has been designed for use by health professionals managing cancer pain in primary care and institutional settings including acute hospitals and nursing homes.

"Pain is what the patient says it is". Pain remains one of the most common and the most feared of symptoms associated with a diagnosis of cancer.

Pain and advanced cancer are not synonymous: 2/3rd of patients experience pain, but 1/3rd will experience no significant pain throughout the course of their illness. 80% of patients who do experience pain will have more than one pain and not all pains will be caused by cancer. Cancer treatments such as surgery and radiotherapy can also be a cause of pain.

Unfortunately, even today many patients do not receive adequate treatment of their pain. Cancer pains can be simply classified according to their response to opioid drugs and most can be controlled provided an appropriate dose of drug is prescribed. Even very difficult pains can be modified and significantly improved.

Professional uncertainty and reluctance to prescribe morphine remains an important cause of poor pain control even though psychological dependence is rarely a problem in patients using opioids for chronic cancer pain.

Cancer pain is an extremely complex and unpleasant sensation which is influenced by many components. There is always a physical basis, but fears about the future, and emotional and spiritual distress suffered by both the patient and the family can all affect how the person experiences the pain, making it unique to its sufferer. Because of this complexity, cancer pain is best managed by a multi-disciplinary approach, into which the patient is the most important contributor. No person should suffer pain without help and most peoples' pain can be improved to the extent that it, and its treatment, has very little impact on the person's day to day life.

This guidance concentrates on the pharmacological management of cancer pain and acknowledges the Scottish Intercollegiate Guidelines Network publication *Control of Pain in Patients with Cancer*[1].

Many other non-drug techniques, either physical such as transcutaneous nerve stimulation and acupuncture, or psycho-social such as distraction or counselling have also been shown to contribute towards the control of cancer pain. These will be discussed in more depth in a forthcoming second publication from the National Council for Hospice and Specialist Palliative Care Services (NC). This second book will also consider the role which a patient's cultural and family setting may have in influencing the plan agreed for the management of pain, and provide practical information and support for the family and lay carers of people with cancer pain.

The aims of cancer pain management are:

- To achieve a level of pain control which is acceptable to the individual.

- To assess the pain and evaluate the effectiveness of pain management promptly

- To be aware of the components of total pain

- To relieve pain at night and at rest and on movement.

- To provide up to date information on the use of pain relieving drugs to patients and their carers

- To provide support and encouragement for caregivers of patients with cancer pain.

The principles of cancer pain management are:

■ Patient and family participation

■ Collaborative multi-professional approach by health professionals

■ Use of appropriate medications, tailored to each patient, individually given and titrated regularly to relieve and prevent pain

■ Ensuring minimum side effects

■ Continued regular follow-up

■ Early referral to a specialist service if appropriate

■ Equality of access for all in a multicultural society.

When a patient presents with pain the cause should be identified whenever possible. Cancer patients frequently have more than one pain. Each pain should be assessed separately.

NB. Sudden severe pain should be recognised as a medical emergency. Patients should be seen and assessed without delay.

The assessment should involve the following:

- Taking a careful pain history from the patient to include a description of the location, duration and quality of the pain.

  Assessing the effect of the pain on day-to-day activities, for example, whether it interferes with sleeping, eating or movement. Carers may be useful in helping with this assessment.

  A pain chart can be used to record the pain history.

- Assessing the patient's mood, particularly for anxiety and depression, which may influence the pain.

  Psychological assessment should include
  awareness of cultural perceptions and belief systems,
  the meaning of the pain to the patient and family,
  the patient's social and financial circumstances (which can all influence his/her perception of pain).

- Taking a careful analgesic history including:

  present and past medication,

  response to analgesic therapy for each pain identified, and

  the occurrence of side effects.

■ Making an accurate diagnosis of the cause of the pain by complete physical examination and appropriate laboratory and radiological investigations. Sophisticated investigations may be appropriate if the patient is fit enough. Some patients will be too ill for more than a history and a brief examination to be used to guide treatment of the pain.

■ Treating the pain effectively while completing the diagnostic evaluation.

■ Evaluating the effectiveness of therapy given, to elicit any side effects and review the treatment plan. The more severe and uncontrolled the pain, the more frequently the patient should be reviewed.

Over 80% of cancer pains can be effectively managed using analgesic drugs according to the recommendations of the WHO Analgesic Ladder. This concept, used as a framework to guide the tailoring of medication to fit the individual's requirements, still has relevance 16 years after its initial publication. Analgesics must be prescribed regularly to control pain and prevent pain recurring. The oral route of administration remains the simplest, most flexible and probably the most acceptable to patients.

Step 1 – Non-opioid: for Mild Pain.

■ Paracetamol; to a maximum recommended 24hr dose of 4g.

■ NSAID; there is insufficient evidence of differential effectiveness and risk to guide the choice of drug.

All patients should also receive a gastro-protective agent.

Cox 2 inhibitors are effective analgesics and probably cause significantly fewer GI ulcers and bleeds. Their use should be considered in 'at risk' patients.

Step 2 – Opioids for mild to moderate pain

■ Codeine and paracetamol combinations.

Dihydrocodeine and paracetamol combinations.

Maximum 24-hour dose restricted to 2 tabs qid.

■ Codeine 30-60mg 4 hourly either alone or taken in conjunction with a non opioid analgesic.

■ Modified release dihydrocodeine 60-120 mg 12 hourly either alone or taken in conjunction with a non-opioid analgesic.

■ Tramadol; maximum recommended 24hr dose 400mg.

■ Coproxamal (dextropropoxyphene with paracetamol) can be used to a maximum of 12 tablets per 24 hours.

Step 3 – Opioids for moderate to severe pain

Morphine remains the drug of choice. The recent introduction of several other strong opioid preparations allows more control over drug-induced side effects and a degree of patient choice. No drug has been shown to have greater analgesic efficacy. Morphine remains the most cost effective.

Morphine

Starting dose

Usually 5mg-10mg of normal release morphine 4hrly, with the same dose prescribed for 'as required' (prn) rescue.

If the patient is elderly or analgesic naive 2.5-5mg normal release morphine.

The dosing interval may need to be longer than 4 hours for patients with impaired renal function. (See page 16, section C.) The frequency can be gauged clinically by the duration of analgesic effect.

Dose increase

The use of prn administration in addition to regular four hourly normal release morphine will allow the dose to be titrated. The dose can be increased after 24 hrs, by 30 - 50%. Two to 4 days should be allowed between dose increases in the elderly or people with impaired renal or liver function. The prn dose should be increased at the same time and to the same level.

There is no maximum dose for morphine. The dose can be titrated upwards until pain is relieved. Once analgesia has been achieved, the dose of normal release morphine can be converted to a modified release preparation for patient convenience and more stable blood levels. Modified release morphine is available as tablets, granules or capsules which may be swallowed whole, or opened and the contents sprinkled on food. These preparations may be given regularly as 12 hrly or as 24 hrly doses. They are not suitable for managing breakthrough pain.

A normal release preparation should always be prescribed for 'as required' administration.

Alternative strong opioids may be indicated if:

A There is difficulty in achieving adequate pain control without unacceptable side effects. However, most problems can be resolved by adjusting the dose of morphine, using adjuvant drugs or other measures (see page 24).

B The route of administration needs to changed.

C The patient has renal or liver impairment

A

Changing from morphine to an alternative strong opioid has sometimes been called opioid rotation or switching. There is no evidence for superior clinical analgesic efficacy of other strong opioids. However some variation in side effect profiles, pharmacokinetics and delivery routes may provide better tolerability for individual patients.

When changing from one opioid to another the published dose conversion charts act as guidelines only. Some, but not all, build in a dose reduction to allow for incomplete cross-tolerance. Clinical judgement will be necessary in each case. Most dose conversion charts are based on conversions from morphine and experience with the other strong opioids will be needed before practitioners will feel familiar enough to convert directly from one alternative opioid to another.

Diamorphine – The strong opioid of choice for subcutaneous use because of its greater solubility compared with morphine. Oral morphine: sc diamorphine conversion ranges between 2:1 and 3:1. This is because of inter patient variation in the bioavailability of oral morphine.

Fentanyl (Transdermal) – This is a useful alternative when background pain is stable but there are problems with swallowing or absorbing drugs orally, vomiting or with intractable constipation on morphine. Note that:

- The patch is replaced every 3 days. Initial analgesic effect may take up to 12 hours and achieving a steady state up to 36 hours. Following removal of the patch it may take 18 hours for a 50% fall in plasma levels.

- Prescribe normal release morphine for breakthrough pain. *(See Table 1 below.)*

- Laxative requirements may fall

- When changing dose, allow 3 days for reassessment and avoid rapid escalation of patch strength.

- If the pain becomes unstable continue treatment with fentanyl and titrate until pain is relieved with normal release morphine. If subcutaneous medication is required use diamorphine.

- The occasional withdrawal syndrome when converting from oral morphine should be managed with normal release morphine.

Table 1 Simple conversion table for choosing a patch size from normal release morphine titration, and for guiding pm morphine dose when using a patch	4 hourly morphine	Fentanyl Patch
	2.5-20mg	25 mcg/h
	25-35mg	50mcg/h
	40-50mg	75mcg/h
	55-65mg	100mcg/h

Hydromorphone – Alternative opioid available as normal release and modified release capsules (can be sprinkled on food) in dose steps comparable to oral morphine eg 1·3 mg capsule equivalent to 10 mg morphine.

Oxycodone – Alternative available in normal release and modified release formulations. Oxycodone 10mg equivalent to 20mg morphine.

Methadone – Alternative opioid. It is cheap but the pharmacokinetic profile makes it difficult to titrate and use. Therefore, only for specialist use.

Phenazocine is currently not available in the UK. Dextromoramide and oral transmucosal fentanyl citrate are considered in the section on Breakthrough Pain.

Transdermal buprenorphine has only recently been introduced to the UK and chemical experience is limited.

Pethidine and meptazinol are not suitable for use in chronic pain due to cancer.

B

Alternative routes of administration when the oral route is inappropriate or where patients would prefer an alternative are:

Transdermal – fentanyl patch (see above).

Rectal – normal release morphine (equivalent dose to oral).

Subcutaneous – diamorphine, oxycodone by infusion or intermittent injection (see above).

Intramuscular – diamorphine in emergencies for acute pain control (not a normal route).

Sublingual – dextromoramide (see Breakthrough Pain).

Buccal – oral transmucosal fentanyl citrate (see Breakthrough Pain).

Epidural (& intrathecal) – there is still debate about exact indications, use and drugs recommended (usually diamorphine and local anaesthetic). Requires specialist personnel.

Topical applications to ulcerated areas, and intranasal preparations are still experimental.

C.

In renal and liver impairment the safety and efficacy of all opioids can change.

Generally, in moderate to severe renal or severe liver impairment consider:

■ Using a reduced starting dose.

■ Cautiously titrate dose to pain relief, observing closely for side effects.

■ In renal failure, consider fentanyl as only a small amount is renally excreted. Hydromorphone and oxycodone may be better tolerated than morphine

■ In liver failure, all opioids potentially accumulate. In clinical practice this is only a problem in patients with severe liver impairment.

Breakthrough pain (including episodic and incident pain) is regarded as pain occurring on top of background pain which is normally controlled.

Management guidance will depend on whether the breakthrough pain is:

the same as or different from the usual background pain

consistently occurring before the next dose of regular analgesia

responding fully to opioids

episodic in timing, intensity or duration

rapid or slow in onset

related to identifiable events

Breakthrough analgesia is usually prescribed as a normal release opioid in a dose of up to 1/6th of the daily opioid dose. It should always be made available when patients with cancer pain are prescribed regular opioids.

Breakthrough analgesia should take effect in 20–30 minutes. If the dose is ineffective, allow one repeat dose, then fully reassess the patient.

If pain is due to inadequate background analgesia – ie usual pain and responding to prn analgesia – then increase regular analgesic dose sensibly.

If pain is occurring consistently before next regular dose, try increasing dose of regular analgesia. Very occasionally the dose interval may need to be shortened (seek specialist advice).

Often breakthrough pain is episodic, ie variable in timing, duration or intensity and may be different in cause from background pain, and of more than one type.

One variant is incident pain when a particular activity or event such as movement, weight-bearing or a dressing change produces pain when the patient is usually pain-free.

Use analgesia appropriate to the cause, which may include adjuvant drugs, surgery or radiotherapy.

Avoid relying on increasing regular analgesia if background pain is controlled.

Allow variations in strength of dose of prn opioid analgesia, depending on intensity of episodic pain.

When incident pain is predictable eg on movement, pre-dosing with opioids 15-20 minutes beforehand can be helpful.

If normal release morphine is too slow in onset, too prolonged in duration or has unacceptable side-effects, consider using dextromoramide sublingually 2·5-20 mgs or oral transmucosal fentanyl citrate (OTFC) 200-1600 mcgs (both need titration). In supervised settings nitrous oxide/oxygen gas (Entonox) can be helpful for painful procedures.

In a patient who appears to have opioid-induced side-effects, first exclude co-morbidity, eg infection, hypercalcaemia or renal failure and drug interactions.

In the absence of co-morbidity or drug interactions, consider reducing the dose of opioid if pain control is acceptable.

Nausea and vomiting

Nausea and vomiting occurs in 15-30% of patients commencing opioids.

■ All patients commencing opioids for moderate to severe pain should have access to an anti-emetic.

■ Opioid-induced nausea and vomiting may be temporary and so anti-emetic use should be reviewed.

■ No studies suggest the superiority of one anti-emetic regimen over another.

■ Commonly used regimens are:
haloperidol 1.5-3mg nocte
cyclizine 50mg 8 hourly
metoclopramide 10-20mg 6 hourly.

Opioid-induced nausea and vomiting is unlikely to develop once a patient is settled on a stable dose of opioids and alternative causes should be investigated.

Constipation

Incidence 40-90%.

No studies suggest the superiority of one laxative regimen over another.

It is recommended that all patients commenced on opioids for moderate to severe pain should be prescribed both softening and stimulant laxatives

■ Commonly used regimens are:
sodium docusate and senna or bisacodyl
lactulose or magnesium hydroxide and senna or bisacodyl
combination preparations such as Codanthramer and
Codanthrusate+Movicol (xtra)

Stimulant laxatives should be used with caution in patients at risk of bowel obstruction

All combination products containing danthron may cause perianal discoloration or a sore rash and should be used with caution in the incontinent patient.

Central nervous system side-effects

Sedation

Patients and their carers should be warned that this may occur in 20-60% of people. Tolerance to this side-effect should develop over a few days.

■ If sedation persists dose reduction should be considered.

■ If dose reduction is unsuccessful then patients may benefit from a switch to an alternative opioid.

■ There is some evidence to suggest that psychostimulants may be helpful but in view of side-effects their use should be supervised by a specialist.

Cognitive impairment

Mild cognitive impairment is common after initiation or dose escalation of opioids. Tolerance to this side-effect usually develops over a few days.

Opioids may lead to confusion or agitated delirium. Should this occur in a patient previously on a stable opioid dose, then renal function should be checked to exclude renal impairment leading to accumulation of opioid metabolites. Management strategies are based on anecdotal evidence and include

■ Opioid dose reduction – if this is unsuccessful then patients may benefit from a switch to an alternative opioid and commencing haloperidol for cognitive impairment.

■ Benzodiazepines for patients with agitated delirium.

Driving

There was no difference in the driving skills of patients on a stable dose of an opioid for moderate to severe pain compared to age and sex matched controls[3]. Patients are usually advised not to drive for a few days after initiation or dose escalation of opioids.

Dry mouth

Incidence up to 20%.

Good mouth care should be encouraged.

Patients may benefit from artificial saliva preparations or stimulants.

Urinary retention

Uncommon, but may occur with opioids, particularly given via the spinal route

Respiratory depression

Very rare if opioids are titrated as recommended.

Pre-existing airways disease is not a contraindication to the use of opioids.

May occur with strong opioids if pain relief is rapidly achieved by other means, eg neural blockade.

Tolerance

Tolerance does develop to some of the side effects of opioids such as sedation and nausea and vomiting.

Tolerance to the analgesic effects of opioids is rare.

If increasing doses are required to maintain pain control, this is usually suggestive of disease progression.

Opioid withdrawal

Opioid withdrawal symptoms may occur if a regular opioid is withdrawn suddenly.

Symptoms include diarrhoea, abdominal cramps, nausea, sweating, shivering and agitation.

Transient withdrawal symptoms have been reported in up to 10% of patients changing from oral morphine to transdermal fentanyl.

Symptoms can be managed with normal release morphine as necessary.

Adjuvant analgesics (or co-analgesics) are drugs that contribute to pain relief in certain situations without being classical analgesics. They are usually used in combination with the analgesics mentioned above.

Some pains will not completely respond to opioid analgesics and will require additional treatments. These may include adjuvant analgesics and anti-cancer treatments. The possibility of achieving pain relief through a response to palliative chemotherapy, hormonal therapy or radiotherapy should always be considered.

It should be remembered that not all pains in a person with cancer are caused by the cancer. Other appropriate diagnosis specific therapy should be considered eg antibiotics for infection or anti-anginals for myocardial ischaemia.

The requirement for opioid analgesia should be regularly reviewed as effective palliation by these treatments may result in reduced requirement and overdosing.

Visceral pain

Corticosteroids are useful for patients with painful hepatomegaly, and for headache from raised intra-cranial pressure. Dexamethasone 4-8mg o.d. as an initial dose is commonly used.

Bone pain

Radiotherapy and NSAIDs are often effective for malignant bony pain.

Corticosteroids (eg prednisolone, dexamethasone) may help generalised bone pain due to metastases.

Bisphosphonates (eg clodronate, pamidronate, zoledronic acid) reduce pain from bone metastases as well as reducing the incidence of painful complications (eg fractures)[4].

Neuropathic pain (Nerve pain)

In cancer-related neuropathic pain, nerve compression or nerve irritation from tumour-induced inflammation may be present, and non-neuropathic pain may co-exist. The pain may respond to opioids and NSAIDs. Corticosteroids are also helpful, especially for patients with severe acute-onset pain, and/or short prognosis.

Tricyclic antidepressants (eg amitriptyline, imipramine) are effective for neuropathic pain; low doses 10-25mg daily may be sufficient[2] but the dose can be titrated against side-effects up to full antidepressant dose. The effectiveness of newer antidepressants (eg SSRIs, SNRIs) is less clear.[5]

Anticonvulsants also have proven efficacy against neuropathic pain. Carbamazepine has the greatest body of supportive evidence, but may cause significant side-effects. Gabapentin, sodium valproate, phenytoin, and clonazepam are also used. Normal anticonvulsant doses are usually used.[6]

Antidepressants and anticonvulsants may be synergistic when used together. There is little to choose between these two groups as first choice.

A large number of other adjuvant analgesics are used in neuropathic pain: ketamine, mexiletine, flecainide, lidocaine (sc infusions), capsaicin cream, baclofen, clonidine, and cannabinoids (cannabis derivatives). These should be initiated by someone with specialist experience.

For some neuropathic pains eg chest wall pain, spinal nerve root compression, pancreatic pain, it is appropriate to refer to specialists pain clinics for neural blockade, TENS etc.

In patients having pain relieving procedures such as nerve blocks it is recommended that the patient's modified release opioid is changed to a normal release preparation prior to the procedure in order to respond quickly to altered analgesic requirements.

Musculo-skeletal pain

Often responds to paracetamol, NSAIDs, relaxation techniques, local heat.

Musculo-skeletal pain may be caused or exacerbated by skeletal muscle spasm, and can be treated with muscle relaxants (eg baclofen, dantrolene, diazepam). (See section on incident pain.)

Smooth muscle colic (intestinal colic, bladder spasms, oesophageal spasm)

Antimuscarinic antispasmodic (eg hyoscine butylbromide, glycopyrronium, propantheline) are used for intestinal colic. Hyoscine hydrobromide crosses the blood-brain barrier and may cause sedation and confusion.

Other antimuscarinics with some selectivity of action may be used for bladder spasms (eg oxybutynin, tolterodine).

Nitrates or calcium channel blockers (eg nifedipine) may help oesophageal spasm.

Regular audit should be an integral part of the implementation of clinical guidelines.

Arrangements, which include a designated individual with responsibility for monitoring, should be in place.

A standard should be agreed, eg reduction in pain to levels acceptable to the patient within 3 days

If this standard is not met, a specialist palliative care team should be consulted.

References

1. Control of Pain in Patients with Cancer. SIGN Publication No. 44. ISBN 1899893 17 2. Published June 2000

2 Strategies to manage the adverse effects of oral morphine: an evidence-based report. Cherny N, Ripamonti C, Pereira J, Fallon M, McQuay H, Mercadante S, Pasternak G, Ventafridda V, for the Expert Working Group of the European Association for Palliative Care Research Network. J Clin Oncol;19:2542-2554

3. Vainio, et al. Driving ability in cancer patients receiving long-term morphine analgesia. Lancet 1995 (September 9); 346: 652-53

4. Mannix K, et al. Using bisphosphonates to control the pain of bone metastases: Evidence-based guidelines for palliative care. Palliative Medicine 2000;14:455-61

5. McQuay HJ, et al. A systematic review of antidepressants in neuropathic pain. Pain 1996;68:217-27

6. McQuay H, et al. Anticonvulsant drugs for management of pain: a systematic review. Br Med J 1995;311:1047-52